HAND LETTERING!

A SHOW-HOW GUIDE!

Written & illustrated
by Keith Zoo

ODD DOT • NEW YORK

Hey there!

This **Show-How** gives you the know-how on hand lettering. We've included only the essentials so you can easily master the FUN-damentals. With just a little practice, you'll soon be doodlin' your own creative alphabet. Ready? Let's go!

MATERIALS NEEDED:

PAPER
(PLAIN, GRID, OR GRAPH PAPER)

RULER *(OR ROLLING RULER)*

ERASER

DRAWING TOOLS *(WHATEVER YOU FEEL COMFORTABLE WITH)*:

PENCILS

PENS

BRUSH-PENS

MARKERS

BRUSHES

WATERCOLORS

CRAYONS

TABLE OF CONTENTS

GETTING STARTED

Hand lettering is all about drawing letters and words, then putting them together to make a piece of art. Don't think of it as writing sentences but as creating really well-designed words or phrases. We'll start by introducing some basic terms used throughout the book:

Cap Line (C) - the top of a capital letter

X Line (X) - roughly the top of a lowercase letter

Base Line (B) - the bottom of both a capital and lowercase letter

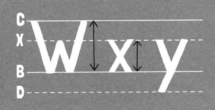

Descender Line (D) - the bottom part of a letter that extends past the base line

TIP: You can change the size and appearance of your letters if you add more or less space between the lines.

If you are using blank paper, you'll need to make sure your lines are straight and parallel. Using a ruler or roller ruler, measure the distance between lines, and use a pencil to draw them. Graph or grid paper is helpful if you want to skip this step.

1

SERIF

WHAT IS SERIF?
You've likely noticed that some letters have lines that come off the tops and bottoms. They look kind of like little feet or hands. Those are called serifs!

Here's an example!

This serif letter A looks as if it's wearing little skis. You can get this look by adding a few strokes to the end of a line.

There are a lot of different ways to make serif letters. Here are a few more examples:

S Straight strokes similar to the example above, with varied thick & thin widths

E Blocky, chunky, straight lines with consistent widths

R Thin & curly lines

I Combination of very thick & very thin lines

F Rounded corners with varied thick & thin widths

How to draw a capital serif letter A:

1. Draw an upside-down V from base line to cap line

2. Draw another diagonal line a few millimeters to the right

3. Connect the top lines & draw a line across the middle

4. Draw two horizontal lines on base line

5. Round out the corners

6. Fill in the letter to finish

A SERIF ALPHABET

Aa Bb Cc

Dd Ee Ff

Gg Hh Ii

Jj Kk Ll

Mm Nn Oo

Pp Qq Rr

Ss Tt Uu

Vv Ww Xx

Yy Zz

2

SANS SERIF

WHAT IS SANS SERIF?
Sans serif makes up a LOT of the letters you see
in the world. The biggest defining feature is the
lack of serifs, hence the name "sans serif."
("Sans" is French for "without"!)

Here's an example!

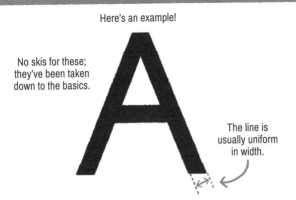

No skis for these; they've been taken down to the basics.

The line is usually uniform in width.

There are a lot of different ways to make sans serif letters. Here are a few more examples:

S   Thin lines, uniform in width

A   Narrow, with very thin & curved lines

N   Thick & chunky

S   Tapered lines with varied thick & thin widths

How to draw a capital sans serif letter A:

C ―――――――――――――――――――――――――――

X ――――――――――――――――――――――――――――

B ――――――――――――――――――――――――――――

D ――――――――――――――――――――――――――――

1. Draw two diagonal lines from base line to cap line & connect

2. Draw two more diagonal lines from cap line to base line & connect

C ―――――――――――――――――――――――――――

X ――――――――――――――――――――――――――――

B ――――――――――――――――――――――――――――

D ――――――――――――――――――――――――――――

3. Draw two horizontal lines in the center

4. Fill in the letter to finish

A SANS SERIF ALPHABET

Aa Bb Cc

Dd Ee Ff

Gg Hh Ii

Jj Kk Ll

Mm Nn Oo

Pp Qq Rr

Ss Tt Uu

Vv Ww Xx

Yy Zz

3

SCRIPT

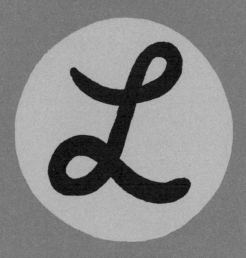

WHAT IS SCRIPT?
Script is the most common form of hand lettering because it works so well with ink, brush-pens, and watercolor. Script letters can flow into one another, creating ornate loops and swirls. Line thickness varies with the direction of your line. Drawing downward (called a downstroke) is often thick. Drawing upward (called an upstroke) is often thin.

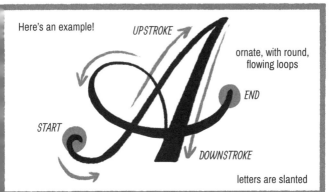

Here's an example!

UPSTROKE

ornate, with round, flowing loops

END

START

DOWNSTROKE

letters are slanted

There are a lot of different ways to make script letters.
Here are a few more examples:

 Thick downstrokes, thin upstrokes with ornate ends

 Varied thick & thin widths with curved ends

 Uniform thin lines with loopy ends

 Extreme thick & thin widths with tapered ends

 Thick downstrokes, thin upstrokes with sharp ends

TIP!

Imagine your letters are blowing in the breeze.

 A combo of thick & thin lines with loops

How to draw a capital script letter A:

C
X
B
D

1. Draw a tapered straight line from base line to cap line

2. Draw a wavy line from cap line to base line

3. Draw a tapered curl at the bottom of the wavy line

C
X
B
D

4. Begin a loop

5. Extend the loop up & over to the right

6. Add another tapered curl to finish

A SCRIPT ALPHABET

Aa Bb Cc

Dd Ee Ff

Gg Hh Ii

Jj Kk Ll

Mm Nn Oo

Pp Qq Rr

Ss Tt Uu

Vv Ww Xx

Yy Zz

4

OUTLINE

WHAT IS AN OUTLINE?
An outline is the outer edge of a shape,
object, or, in this case, a letter!

TIP: When you trace an outline of your hand, it doesn't look exactly like your hand. Your letters don't have to look perfect, either!

Outlines can be used on any of the styles we've practiced so far.

Here are some samples for serif, sans serif, and script.

SERIF

SANS SERIF

SCRIPT

TIP: You can change the thickness of your outline to be really thin or really thick!

How to draw a capital, outline, sans serif letter A:

C
X
B
D

1. Use a pencil to draw an upside-down V from X line to base line

2. Draw a line on either side from cap line to base line

3. Draw two lines in the middle

C
X
B
D

4. Erase the center lines as shown

5. Connect the top lines on cap line

6. Connect the bottom lines at base line to finish

AN OUTLINE ALPHABET

Aa   Bb   Cc

Dd   Ee   Ff

Gg   Hh   Ii

Jj Kk Ll

Mm Nn Oo

Pp Qq Rr

Ss Tt Uu

Vv Ww Xx

Yy Zz

5

BUBBLE

WHAT IS A BUBBLE LETTER?
A bubble letter is very similar to an outline letter, but we'll add some elements to make the letters look more like they are made of bubbles!

Imagine this letter A is coming right off a bubble wand.

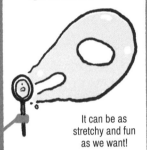

It can be as stretchy and fun as we want!

To give the appearance of it being a bubble, we want to add highlights.

TIP: To get the look you want, you might need to fill it in with a color.

Bubbles are big and round, so we want to keep the letter looking similar.

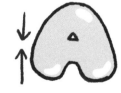

OR

TIP: Stretch and squish each letter until you get it the way you want. The thicker it gets, the chunkier the bubble will look.

21

How to draw a capital, bubble, sans serif letter A:

C
X
B
D

1. Draw a rounded upside-down U shape

2. Draw a small U shape with a curl at the top

3. Repeat the small U shape to connect the bottom

C
X
B
D

4. Draw a small circle in the center

5. Draw the bubble highlights

6. Fill in around the highlight shapes to finish

A BUBBLE LETTER ALPHABET

Aa Bb Cc

Dd Ee Ff

Gg Hh Ii

Jj Kk Ll

Mm Nn Oo

Pp Qq Rr

Ss Tt Uu

Vv Ww Xx

Yy Zz

6

DROP SHADOW

WHAT IS A DROP SHADOW?
A drop shadow can give your lettering a cool
effect to look as if it's floating or lit up.

Look at this drop shadow of Tod!

Try imagining light shining from the top right. All the shadows will be cast to the bottom left.

Try another angle, with the letter lit from the bottom left.

Now flip it and try an angle from the top left.

Try filling in spaces of your drop shadow to create a 3-D effect!

How to draw a capital, drop shadow, sans serif letter A:

C ———————————————————
X ———————————————————
B ———————————————————
D ———————————————————

1. Draw two diagonal lines from base line to cap line & connect

2. Draw two more diagonal lines from cap line to base line & connect

3. Draw two horizontal lines in the center

C ———————————————————
X ———————————————————
B ———————————————————
D ———————————————————

4. Fill in the letter

5. Draw a shadow outline in the direction of the light

6. Fill in the shadow to finish

A DROP SHADOW ALPHABET

Aa Bb Cc

Dd Ee Ff

Gg Hh Ii

Jj Kk Ll

Mm Nn Oo

Pp Qq Rr

Ss Tt Uu

Vv Ww Xx

Yy Zz

7

PATTERN

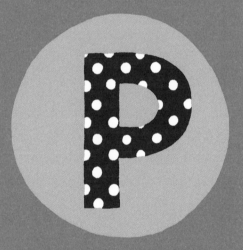

WHAT IS A PATTERN?
A pattern is a repeated decorative design or
element that you can draw inside your letters.

Here are some examples of common patterns:

 TIP! Think about how your favorite patterned shirt looks, then use that as inspiration!

How to draw a capital, pattern, serif letter A:

C
X
B
D

1. Draw two diagonal lines from base line to cap line & connect

2. Draw two more diagonal lines from cap line to base line & connect

3. Draw two horizontal lines in the center

C
X
B
D

4. Draw two rectangles on the base line

5. Fill in empty spaces & choose a pattern

6. Paint or draw the pattern over the letter to finish

A PATTERN ALPHABET

Jj Kk Ll

Mm Nn

Oo Pp Qq

Rr Ss Tt

Uu Vv Ww

Xx Yy Zz

TIP: Try this technique with other fonts like bubble or script!

8

KAWAII

WHAT IS KAWAII?
In Japan, this word can be used to describe all
sorts of adorable things—including letters.

You'll need plenty of room inside each letter for your face, so keep the letters big and bold.

For this reason, we'll be creating only the uppercase version of the letters.

Softening the edges will give it a friendlier vibe.

To find a good spot for a face, imagine the letter shape is a head or body.

Add some eyes and a mouth, some rosy cheeks, and maybe even an accessory!

If you're struggling to come up with an idea for a face, think about what emotion you want to convey.

HAPPY

CONFIDENT

UPSET

EXCITED

NERVOUS

CONTENT

MISCHIEVOUS

CRYING

GOOFY

SCARED

AWESTRUCK

COOL

GRUMPY

LAUGHING

SHOCKED

How to draw a capital, kawaii, sans serif letter A:

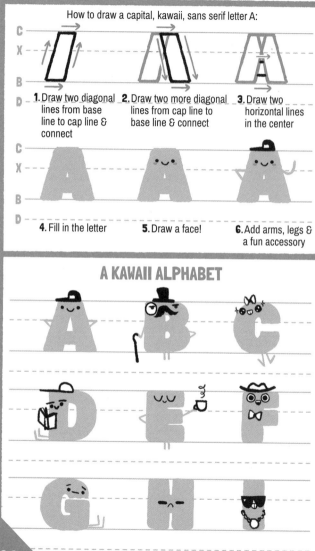

1. Draw two diagonal lines from base line to cap line & connect

2. Draw two more diagonal lines from cap line to base line & connect

3. Draw two horizontal lines in the center

4. Fill in the letter

5. Draw a face!

6. Add arms, legs & a fun accessory

A KAWAII ALPHABET

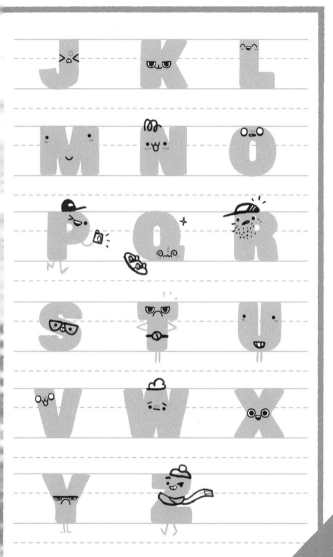

9
MONSTER

WAIT, DID YOU SAY "MONSTER"?

Yep! We'll make our very own MONSTER ALPHABET.

Start by thinking of what kind of monster you want it to be.

A creepy-crawly? You could try a thin letter and make it look squiggly or slimy.

A big fuzz ball? Try making your letter nice and thick, then add fur!

Ooh, that looks fun! Let's keep going and add some eyeballs, a mouth, and some horns. Try coloring it in, too!

How to draw a capital, monster, sans serif letter A:

C
X
B
D

1. Sketch diagonal lines with a pencil as shown

2. Connect the lines, rounding the corners

3. Sketch two horizontal lines in the middle

C
X
B
D

4. Use a pen to place features as if the letter were a body or head

5. Use a pen to make monstery outlines (fur, slime, etc.), then erase pencil underneath

6. Fill it in with a color!

For this example, we've combined monstery uppercase with slimy lowercase.

Aa Bb Cc

Dd Ee Ff

Gg Hh Ii

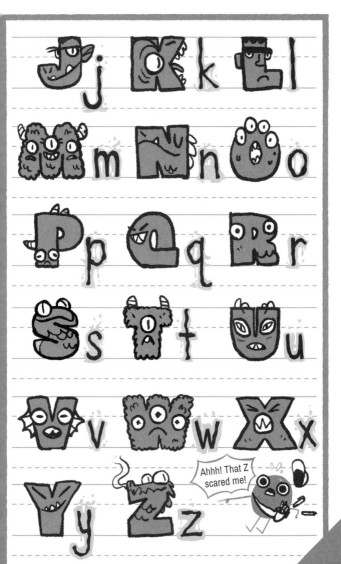

Ahhh! That Z scared me!

10
ALL TOGETHER

COMBINE TECHNIQUES TO CREATE FUN STUFF!

Packaging

Hand lettering is found on logos, signs, product packaging, greeting cards, video games, gift bags, book covers . . .

. . . EVERYWHERE! Look around—can you find some hand lettering examples? Let's practice combining techniques on the next few pages!

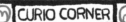

ZOO'S

CURIO CORNER

GAMES · COLLECTIBLES

MAKE A LOGO!

Let's hand letter a logo. Start by picking a theme. Choose something that interests you. In this example, we're using cereal. (Because, why not?) So let's make a logo for our cereal box.

Try writing the word *cereal* in different ways. For example, here is the word written with a crunchy texture pattern and in outline. It looks like actual pieces of cereal!

TEXT ON A PATH

Sometimes things look more interesting if they are not on a straight line, especially on cereal boxes.

Try drawing a curved line and use it as a guide for drawing your letters. The path can be the base and cap lines of each letter, giving your word more flavor!

ILLUSTRATIONS

Since cereal boxes are fun, let's add some illustrations to go along with our lettering!

A bowl, crunchy cereal, a spoon, and milk will all be great props.

BORDERS

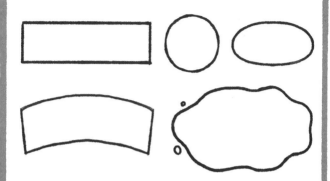

Bring everything together by creating a border around your word. For example, a blob of spilled milk would make a pretty cool border for this cereal logo.

FINISH IT OFF!

Combine all your ideas into one image to create a logo!

TIP: Designers often make many different versions of the same logo before they settle on a favorite. Try making as many different logos as you can think of!

THINK OF WORDS THAT ARE OPPOSITES

Try giving the letters the characteristics of what the word means. *Scary* could have really thin, creepy letters, while *calm* could look very still and rigid.

Play with the sizes of letters and words.

Add additional elements to play off what your word means. Add some props or special effects.

COMBINE WORDS AND LOCATIONS

This can be an easy way to generate some really cool ideas for trying out your new techniques. Take a word and a location and combine them in interesting ways.

Jekyll's MONSTER "FACTORY"

Go one step further and add a name, too!

LETTER SPACING

The space between your letters is important. If they are too far apart, the letters won't read as a word!

Now that the letters are closer together, it reads as the word *The*.

Bonus Fact: When two letters meet like this *T* and *h*, it's called a *ligature*.

Or take it one step further. You can get fancy with the way you connect letters! These letters connect with loops, which is one way to use your script skills!

46

TOOLS & TECHNIQUES

Here's a fun (and efficient) way to practice different techniques using a drawing pad, pencil, tracing paper, tape, and other drawing tools like markers and paints.

1 DRAW!

Sketch out your designs on paper with pencil first.

2 USE TRACING PAPER!

When you get close to something you like, tape a piece of tracing paper on top and trace your design, redrawing the areas you want to fix. If you don't have tracing paper, hold both pages up against a window.

3 EXPERIMENT (A LOT)

You can place all kinds of different papers on top of your original design and trace over it with markers, paints, inks, or whatever you want to use! The more you practice, the easier it will get!

4 USE DIFFERENT TYPES OF TOOLS

Depending on what you want your hand lettering to look like, there are a lot of different types of tools. Brush-pens and paintbrushes will help you get varied thick and thin widths. Markers and pens will give you a nice, consistent width.

An imprint of Macmillan Publishing Group, LLC
120 Broadway, New York, NY 10271
OddDot.com

Library of Congress Cataloging-in-Publication Data is available.
ISBN 978-1-250-24999-9

Editor: Justin Krasner
Cover designer: Colleen AF Venable & Tim Hall
Interior designer: Colleen AF Venable & Tae Won Yu

Our books may be purchased in bulk for promotional,
educational, or business use. Please contact your local bookseller
or the Macmillan Corporate and Premium Sales Department at
(800) 221-7945 ext. 5442 or by email at
MacmillanSpecialMarkets@macmillan.com.

Show-How Guides is a trademark of Odd Dot.
Printed in China by Hung Hing Off-set Printing Co. Ltd., Heshan City,
Guangdong Province
First edition, 2020

10 9 8 7 6 5 4 3 2 1

DISCLAIMER
The publisher and author disclaim responsibility
for any loss, injury, or damages that may
result from a reader engaging in the
activities described in this book.

Keith Zoo

is an artist and illustrator living in Massachusetts. You can find more of his work at keithzoo.com and on Instagram @keithzoo.